THE SUNRISE FLOW

To all those who've felt the burden of the **darkest** nights, who have searched for their own sunrise, this book is **for you**. It's for the ones who've discovered that the path to that sunrise **begins** by getting in tune with your own soul, by letting your **heart's rhythm** guide you like a river's gentle flow.

This book is dedicated to the courageous **souls who've dared** to be themselves, who've been persistent to over**come the** life's challenges despite the storms of opinion that tried to **bring them down**. It's for those who've taken life one step at a time, **understanding** that each step is a part of the beautiful journey.

To all those who've ever been made to feel **like they** weren't enough, this book is especially for you. It's for the **times when** you've been emotionally drained, yet you've found the **strength** to carry on.

May these pages be your best friend, a com**forting** companion on your path. May you find your happy home in **these words**. May the verses within remind you that you are not alone, **and that** your journey, no matter how challenging, is a beautiful one.

With love and understanding.

THE

Sunrise

FLOW

JASKIRAN MANGAT

CONTENTS

CHAPTER 2: A JOURNEY INWARDS

CHAPTER 3: RESILIENCE RISING

CHAPTER 4: THE LIGHT WITHIN

You surely see the sunrise conquering the darkness.
being in flow with yourself.

So. let you be you.

THE SUNRISE FLOW

INTRODUCTION

In the realm of poetry, where words hold the power to echo emotions and let them flow freely, get ready to begin your journey of self-discovery and self-love alongside the remarkable woman at the heart of this book. As you hold these pages in your hands, you're about to step into her world, traversing the path as she seeks her sunrise, confronts challenges with resilience, and embraces her self-worth. This book stands as a testament to her strength—a collection of verses that weave together a tapestry of unique yet familiar human sentiments. It's a world where emotions flow freely.

As you dive into this journey, you may find yourself resonating with her emotions and experiences. The verses within offer a ray of hope, light, and inspiration. They are a reminder, no matter how dark the night is, you will eventually experience an exquisite sunrise gracing your horizon. This book aspires to introduce you to your own flow of sunshine.

The book's origin lies in the author's words:

"Her actions were not a mere act but a regard for expressing the beauty of her kind soul."

This verse reflects the journey of a strong and courageous woman who, at one point, found herself entangled in constant battles and lost in the judgments imposed upon her. As her existence began to fade amidst the intricacies of her own thoughts, she realized the importance of being kind to herself, not jeopardizing her own emotions and well-being. Over time, as she took small steps in her journey, newfound self-love began to pour her way, allowing her to discover her own sunrise flow. This echoed that each step taken towards self-love is an acknowledgement of her emotions and honour for a beautiful soul.

This book isn't merely a reflection of one woman's journey: it's a reflection of human emotions. Each poem is a path to sunrise, each ray radiates the light of persistence, overcoming negative thoughts, and discovering inner power. Allow these words to inspire you, let them guide you, and remind that you have the potential to find your inner light unveiling your own sunrise.

Let's delve into a world of deepest emotions to locate the keys to unlock our innermost being. This journey is split into different chapters portraying the emotions of our protagonist at different stages of self-discovery.

"In Her Own Words: Introduction to Her World" sets the stage for this journey. It's an intimate outlook into the soul of our protagonist – where she is ready to dream, accept her strengths and flaws, enjoy her passions and embrace her spirit.

"A Journey Inwards: Struggles with Self-Love" recites the emotional distress with self-doubt and insecurity. Here, we witness her battles with the darkest of thoughts which cloud the divine light. The verses reflect her struggles, intimate conversation with mind and the soul discovering the inner conflicts that all too often obstruct her from listening to her true voice.

"Resilience Rising: Overcoming Hardships" is a tale of strength within. We explore the journey of her perseverance as she goes on to be her own inspiration. This chapter reminds us that no matter the life's storms, you hold the enough power to overcome it all with own mindset.

"Finding Light Within: Embracing Self-Love" celebrates triumph of self-love over adversity as she eventually discovers her sunrise. Here, we applaud her victory in embracing self-love, and coming back to life stronger with compassion and self-acceptance.

Traversing through the journey, you will find "A Subtle Reminder: A Poem of Renewal" which offers moments of reflection, an opportunity to pause and absorb the wisdom.

As you turn these pages, let these poems be your companion to help navigate the intricacies of life, as you confront your own struggles. As you embark on this poetic journey, remember that these words are not just letters on a page; they are the light guiding your way, whispers of encouragement, and echoes of your own resilience. May this book be a guiding light on your path to self-discovery, self-love, and unwavering persistence. May you find your own sunrise flow in these verses, may you find hope, and courage to let your own light shine, illuminating your unique path.

introduction to her world

ORDINARY

She's ordinary as a being,
yet, rare in her perception.
Discrete core of her existence
is the treasure she carries,
the rest is all
just a misconception.

Excitement of her dreams,
the serenity of heart
is what she embodies,
though, what world sees
is only a part.

Distinction she holds within, sets her free,
still, she is ordinary as any being.

HER EXISTENCE

The first sight of her presence,
enchant into a graceful warmth so divine.
The depth of her eyes,
mirror the spark of innate courage
and passion that forever strive.
A glance at her enticing smile,
reminds that there remains
a profound innocence still alive.
The expression of her vivid emotions,
unearth new dimensions of existence
far beyond the ability of
mere words to describe.

a poem of renewal

DIVINE PEACE

Embracing the reality,
life is like a bubble.
Winding through this journey,
we all endeavour to fit
pieces of our own puzzle.
Still, as life unrolls
learn to cherish the walk,
adorn it with the fragrance of memories
to welcome the divine peace,
it finally unlocks.

LET IT FLOW

She's mature, yet silly,
She's silent, yet loud,
She's smart, still sometimes an idiot,
She's chaotic, yet in harmony,
She's realistic, but hysterical in love,
She's passionate, yet at peace with little things,
There is no defined either or,
She's everything that she enjoys.
Why try to fit into a mould,
when she can live a life in a moment
and simply let it flow.

LOVE FOR DANCE

In rhythm with melody
her body flows,
with each step
serenity and elegance bestows.
Oblivious to the mundane reality
solely in passion,
wholly cherishing
the warmth and compassion.

The courage embodies
as she reaches the sky,
brilliance radiates resilience
impossible to defy.
Leaving a trail of inspiration
she rests to ground,
unleashing a grace
in presence so profound.

a poem of renewal

THE MATURITY

You embrace the maturity,
when nostalgia stirs.
The blunders of the past
no longer concern.
Rather the lessons learned
impart an astounding grace
along with the kindness it infers.

THE ECHO

*S*he never knew what she wanted,
but well aware of what she did not.
These well versed thoughts echo,
whenever she sense her world tearing apart.
This understanding in itself
has proved to be enough,
to keep her going
even when the days've been tough.

TRUTH OF SOUL

The existence of her eyes **searching** the sky,
seeking the sacred truth **of her** why.
She is onto a journey to **be unwind,**
where her essence she **would find.**
She's determined to embr**ace the** quest,
to realize the truth of **her soul,**
embracing the gratificati**on it attests.**
Wandering through **the path,**
she is setting her **ways,**
to ultimately discover her **sunshine** rays.

a poem of renewal

SOLITUDE

Solitude is a peace of mind,
a form of stillness,
self acceptance and soulful love,
when accepted
with an open heart.

A QUESTION

in her own words

Someone asked
"why are you quiet? "
She answered
"because at times
before being heard, I rather
listen and connect with
my intrinsic voice."

A RARE ESSENCE

You may unfold her mind and soul,
she'll still own a piece of her essence
which nobody is aware of.
You may criticize her spirit or extol,
nevertheless she'll fully embrace herself
for she is well conscious of her whole
and what she brings to the world.

a poem of renewal

NO PERFECT

There exists no perfect time,
To seize that opportunity.

A seed found no perfect soil to sprout,
Yet with persistence, conformed to grow.

A flower fretted, it hasn't bloomed perfect,
Still a moth relished its presence.

There is no perfect defined love,
But, an affection embracing the true souls.

No moment you breathe in is perfect,
While emotions you cherish are.

There ain't a perfect you,
Only a matter enclosing strengths and flaws.

There ain't no perfect human,
So, lets be gracious to yourself and all.

the story of struggles

FAR AWAY

a journey inwards

She always wanted to stay
but couldn't.
For once, she's been a chaos
that needed to discern stillness
hidden deep in the soul's
darkest of ways.
At times, to reach there
one needs to
wander through the places far away.

A NIGHTMARE

In the uncanny world of ordeal,
while standing strong
her soul felt captivated by storm.
With every passing moment,
the exhausting wind she breathes
affirms its not where she belongs.

Guided by the depth of her thoughts,
she gathers the courage
unveiling a divine light.
As she gasped into reality,
her drowsy eyes awake
remembering there remains
an ambition yet to create.

Following the vision,
the guiding echoes resound,
as she embarks on a journey
to unleash the harmony abound.

a poem of renewal

FATE VS FAITH

Unaltered by the fate,
what matters is the abounding faith
in your intrinsic truth, abilities,
and the forever dream.
This faith when embraced,
embody force so profound
that it'll be destined
to reach your aims,
no matter how extreme.

INEVITABLE LIFE

One day she is full of life,
while others entirely empty.

At times, her heart soars high,
while others it simply cries.

For moments, there is endless to say,
then, deep silence as nothing remains.

Nevertheless how strongly you seek,
life inevitably is no sole entity
rather an amalgam of emotions,
both strong and weak.

Either ways,
when life happens
just embrace your soul,
and shower yourself with kind love
that indeed you deserve.

DEFINING HER

At times, she couldn't
define herself in mere **words**,
nor did anyone understand
often leading to an imminent pain.
Thus, one day she stopped defining
rather began creating **a journey**,
portraying her actions with **sheer** integrity
renouncing any need to explain.

a poem of renewal

PAST IS BEHIND

a subtle reminder

Healing isn't about forgetting
situations, places and people,
but simply accepting that
your existence is beyond the past.
Folding into your arms
unveil a self compassion that forever lasts.
Indifferent to what others opine,
let your hidden faith thrive.
Residing in that deep found love
with your beautiful soul,
persist to be gentle and kind.

UNWIND

Her mind kept wandering,
engrossed in prospective intentions.
She remained, entrapped by the probable,
unconscious to the wearying contentions.

Implied you are a warrior queen,
yet, not all battles are worth the fight.
Somedays you must rejuvenate your soul,
and that rather is equally right.

EVENTUALLY

a journey inwards

Eventually what has fallen out
will come to its place,
the turmoils it has brought
will soon find its calm.
She knows it won't be easy
but keeping faith in herself
she's persistent to lift the spirit high,
to eventually, shed the clouds
that've once brought her the qualm.

a poem of renewal

ESCAPE THE CHATTER

*B*e part of a story,
where you matter.
Confine to conversations
where you are listened to
and accepted at heart,
not for what you can offer.

Be part of a place,
which brings you the peace
and makes you feel at comfort.

Know from your instinct
where you belong
as this world is a busy square
full of unnecessary chatter.

UNTIL SHE COULDN'T

She kept the calm
and constantly tried
until she couldn't.
She allowed the lies
quietly walking her path
until she couldn't.
Well aware of the void
in the reality of her being,
she chose to be unfettered
by worldly chaos and sound,
to build herself a home
far away from objections
where love is pure and abound.
Though, into all this
she chose to be kind
until she finally couldn't.

THE PATTERNS

a journey inwards

She continued to learn
in the hope to find a new self
and not be stale
rather forgot, before all,
she needs to unlearn
the patterns holding her back
which deep down
still prevail.

a poem of renewal

PRESENT

a subtle reminder

Lost in the constant notion
of being content,
we forget to acknowledge
the gratification for
what we are,
and what we have at present.

After all, nothing stays
but the moments we create,
and memories to cherish
is all that matters in the end.

HER WAYS

She's not meant to simply
accept the limiting beliefs
with which she doesn't align.
She rather is willing to follow
the rules she herself has defined.
She's not flustered by judgements
and fiercely expresses,
whatever is in her mind.

The path she's chosen is tied with hurdles
and might be tough.
Owning to her truth, feeling no regrets,
she'd at least be enough.

THE OCEAN

*R*ight in sight of her eyes
she sees an enchanting ocean,
abundant in the vibrancy of
love, cheers and giggles.
In ubiquity of a lively ocean,
it seemed all fair
to also embrace occasional tears.
Thus, she stopped holding it back
rather let it flow
in the vastness of ocean,
for it to mingle with positive experiences
which make the ocean aglow.

a poem of renewal

IS IT FOREVER?

*B*e brave enough to accept
that everyone you meet
is not meant to be forever.
If someone turns their back,
acting as if what you offered
was not enough ever,
don't be fool enough
to pretentiously follow.
Rather, truthfully accept
keep walking your way,
remember, it is imminent that
no matter what you do,
sometimes the world is too hollow.

overcoming hardships

THE LIGHT

She might have been hurt,
but, not broken.
She might have been scarred,
but, not demolished.
She might have been wounded,
but, healed with love abound.
She might have failed hard,
but, embraced courage to continue.
Yes, she the warrior who shines bright,
She might be unaware of the ultimate,
but, she can foresee an unyielding light.

UNBOUNDED HOPE

resilience rising

On the verge of breakdown,
she's determined to pursue hope,
finding an unbounded inspiration,
those hushed dreams once again awoke.

Echoing the newfound affirmations
into the depths of her mind,
she finds an unbounded courage,
guiding her spirit high into the skies.

For within her heart, that inspiration resides,
shattering the storms with her passion
she's once again ready to unwind.

a poem of renewal

EXPECTATIONS

Sometimes its not others,
but you get lost
in your own expectations.
Remember,
aspirations are really worth it,
when lived with a joy
else when forced
it only impose limitations.
If something isn't your way,
don't stop
and keep exploring,
who knows
you'll find better destinations.

WHISPERS & CHEERS

You whisper, I lost a game,
I cheer, I own the battle ahead.
You whisper, the darkness is forever,
I cheer, the light is my way however.
You whisper, I am weak,
I cheer, for the strength within I seek.
You whisper, I am too much,
I cheer, for my uniqueness as such.
You whisper, I make mistakes,
I cheer, for the patterns it breaks.
You whisper, I can't overcome the fear,
I cheer, for the challenges I bear.
You whisper, its a mere luck,
I cheer, for the life I construct.
In the whispers, I hear a choice,
to accept your doubts or listen to my voice.
I choose the latter, to bring my soul light,
For its my story, that I would recite.

BROKEN BUT UNBROKEN

resilience rising

She gathered each of her broken pieces
well aware that it can never be the same,
yet with her stirring fortitude
she can put it all together once again,
to allow herself afresh chances
that had been waiting for her
to embrace and reclaim.

a poem of renewal

WITHIN YOU

There is no such moment
that can define your worth,
There is no such place,
where you can find your worth.
Rather than trying
to find yourself around,
just be you.
Be what you love naturally,
do what brings you inner peace,
and be what's morally humane.
No matter what the world pursues,
you'll not find your worth anywhere,
but only within you.

VIVID NIGHT

In the dimness of night,
when the world goes quiet,
the continued exchange of sentiments
between her heart and mind
is what drives her to a periphery,
where her mind finds a clarity
and her spirit afresh light.

IN THAT PRESENCE

$\mathcal{S}$he felt divine in that presence,
the wandering thoughts came to quiescence.
She unveiled a familiar essence,
in those starry eyes, an aura highly precious.

In her own thoughts, she would stray,
lost in the doubts, questioning her ways.
In that presence, she found the strength,
to embrace her flaws and soul to its depth.

It seemed as she found a key,
newfound connection flourished to set her free.
Embracing the solitude with her grace,
the lost paths she vowed to retrace.

So, in the reflection of her own eyes,
she discovered a scared space in her soul.
In that presence, unveiling a divine light,
though being lone, she still felt whole.

a poem of renewal

THREE SPHERES

If you can provide for yourself,
you are independent.
If you can provide for your loved ones,
you are mature.
If you can provide for others,
you carry a gracious heart.
For each of these,
there is no right or wrong,
rather all diverse spheres of being
where everyone can
and equally deserve to belong.
At last, it merely is a matter of choice
of what you truly want.

IN THAT MOMENT

And in that moment,
she grew into existence,
grasping the enormity of being
which in her realm
seemed far away in distance.

Time halted,
as she reached an impasse,
feeling baffled in her own thought.

Yet, the moment carried its worth,
determined to stay there
she explored,
unveiling the innate wisdom
that she always ignored.
In that instant, she found a clarity,
relishing the truth and
essence of her rarity.

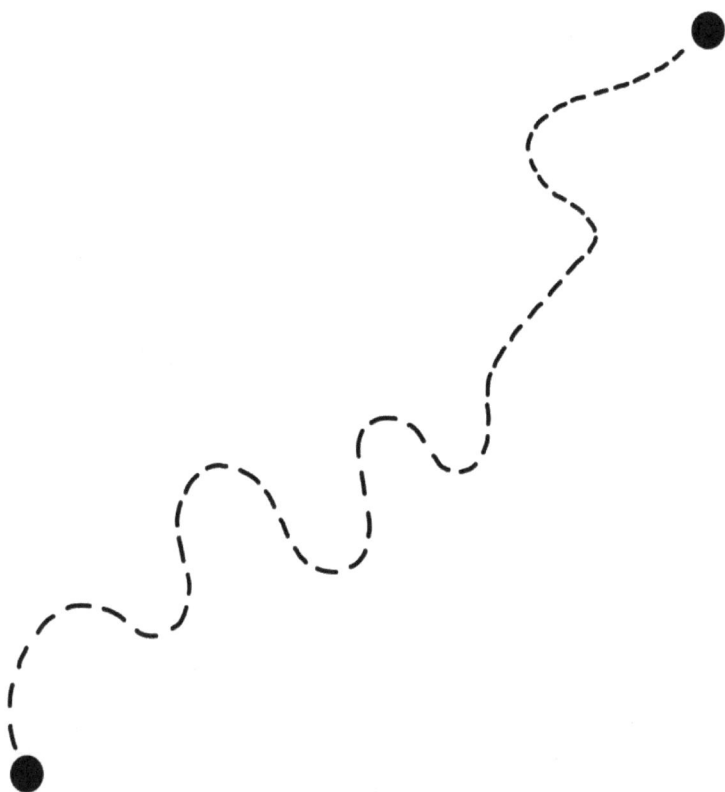

STEP AFTER STEP

It all began with a step
to find a little inspiration,
exploring different ways
to create a life
reflecting her aspirations.
Despite the hurdles on the way,
she decided to keep going,
at times totally unaware of her destination.
It was in fact during this course
that she ended up discovering
the whole new world of her existence
beyond any imagination.

Truly, all it entailed was
taking a step after step.

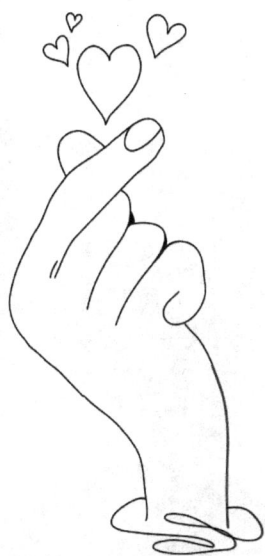

a poem of renewal

LITTLE LOVE

If someday you got only
little love in your heart,
shower it on yourself first,
before you can offer others a part.
Know, its not a reflection of self obsession,
rather a fair dispersal of love
in your possession.
For if you do so,
only then you can fully revive,
to eventually bestow others
a share of love within
that now abundantly thrives.

I CHOOSE

resilience rising

*T*oday I choose myself,
breathe in my utter reality,
refusing to be afflicted
by the expectations imposed.

Today I choose to listen
to my subdued voice,
honour my conscience,
letting my thoughts be exposed.

Today and forever,
I choose myself,
regarding my inner peace,
reconnecting
with the light of my being.

THE STORY

She is onto writing,
her own story
in the way she desires,
not how the world expects it
or requires.

a poem of renewal

MORE THAN ENOUGH

You being here - mere existing
is more than enough
of a reason to love
and being kind to yourself
even when nothing else is.

Your immense love and support
for being authentic you
in every situation
is in itself an achievement
realized by only a few.

HER SUPREMACY

For the sparkle in her eyes,
for an endearing smile,
carrying the grace and warmth
in her own style.
She is on a quest,
to embrace the purpose,
nurture her dreams
to explore her wisdom,
and shatter any norms.

She's a women in her supremacy,
affirming her choice,
honouring her worth and might.
In her uniqueness,
she's found the strength
to withstand the darkest of nights.

a poem of renewal

ABSENCE OF PRESENCE

In the absence of a loving presence,
you'll feel alone,
but,
never let that presence be yours,
or to your own self
you'll become unknown.

triumph of self-love

SIMPLY LET GO

She found a homely place
full of comfort and kindness,
leaving behind all the chase
blooming the essence within,
where only
love is what's embraced.

All it took was to let go,
Let go of unpredictable
and unaligned,
Let go of judgements,
that once confined.
In the symphony of emotions,
simply discover what matters
and let that warmth shine.

ETERNALLY TOGETHER

Amidst the dilemma so **consistent**,
she welcomed her **weary soul**,
with open arms
wiped the precious **tears**
and embraced her **whole**.

In the warmth of heaven**ly** solace,
she finds her soulful **love**,
together laughter **echoes**
as tears begin to **fade**.

Eternally in a sweet **kiss**
healing all the **wounds**,
in enchanting treasures of **toge**therness,
her soul flourish**ed**
in a pure bliss.

a poem of renewal

BREATHE TO EASE

When you feel overwhelmed,
unable to cope with life,
pause there,
deeply inhale,
absorbing the sailing breeze.
Hold on for a moment,
tightly embrace yourself
as you breathe.
Let these futile emotions pass through,
and release any thoughts
putting you to unease.

THE LESSONS

the light within

In life whatever she seeks,
she believes and creates.
Whether its love, respect or passion,
she doesn't cater to demands
rather reciprocates
whats offered to her plate.
She's come to a calm
within her heart and soul.
She surely knows
from the lessons on the way,
what's her will remain,
what's not will eventually fade.
So truly, when she loves,
she just let it grow.
Sincere love one can offer,
she firmly holds.

LOST CHARM

the light within

Once again she's found **her charm**,
which at time was **lost**
somewhere in the **storm**.
Conquering the constant **battles**,
she's come back **to life**
even stronger,
enjoying it with an **utmost calm**.

a poem of renewal

A MOON

When the world seems so afar,
compelling you to feel
that you are the only one
with a perception so bizarre.
Never devalue your core ethical beliefs,
realize that maybe no one is aware,
but you are a moon
in a galaxy full of stars.

ACT OF BEAUTY

Her actions were not a **mere act,**
but a regard to express her **beautiful** soul.
Some regarded it an act, whi**le she** laughed,
knowing in her heart, wh**at they** lost.
Warm love in the heart was w**hat she** embossed,
guiding her conquer the objec**tions others** sought.
For her courage, facing **the odds,**
she's been firm to keep **her calm.**
With strong force in her **fierce** eyes,
she's celebrates her reality, **beyond** those lies.
Her actions spoke louder, rea**lizing** each goal,
she's a women embracing a **beautiful** soul.

A REFLECTION

She started to see
herself rather clearly,
once she started to condone
what world wanted her to believe,
rather fully accept
the brilliance of her own.

a poem of renewal

FINE MOMENTS

The moments you breathe in,
The moments you walk in,
The moments you eat in,
The moments you talk in,
The moments you thrive in,
The moments you learn in,
The moments you fight in,
The moments you survive in,
each moment is precious.
Stop slipping away
these fine moments in
the past's despair
or tomorrow's fear.
Rather start to cherish them,
for each of these moments is rare.

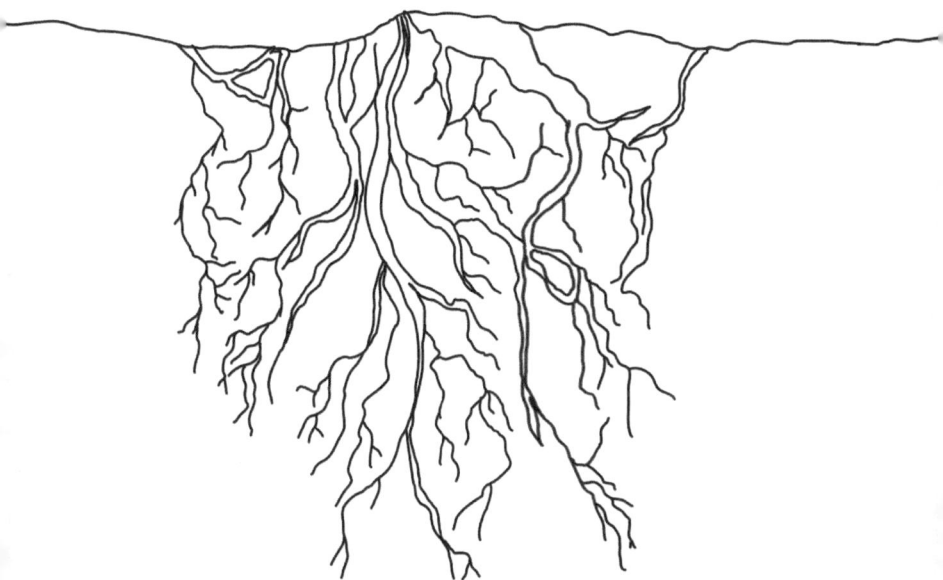

ROOTED IN REALITY

the light within

$\mathcal{R}$ooted through the experiences
she's flourished on her own.
Nurtured with love,
she's build a place within
that can happily be called a home.
Fighting all the odds,
she's come thus far
living the reality of her dreams,
that once she'd imagined
while gazing at the stars.

HER HAPPY PLACE

Amid all that's been unkind
she's always stood her ground,
amongst the wavering crowd.
Only she's been consistent
in providing herself the kindness
that she completely deserves
and herself had vowed.

She assured herself,
consoled herself,
appreciated herself,
and laughed with herself
when no one else did.

In her generosity, she's let go,
by no means making her weak,
rather attesting her determination
to detach from the unpleasant thoughts,
keeping herself in a happy place
that she always seeks.

a poem of renewal

THE ALLIANCES

In an effort to be with new people,
never lose sight of the ones
who have stayed throughout.
Cherishing every bit of your story,
supporting eminently, even when
you were surrounded in doubt.

New relations are never meant to estrange
existing ones, including the one with yourself.

HERE AND NOW

the light within

Here and now she owns her time
to learn, fall and continue to grow.
She's said no to disparaging
her own emotions and thoughts,
rather assured to go with the flow.
She's transcended a long journey
to find a blooming soul,
without any unwieldy expectations
that she owes.
Here and now, kindness for herself
is the only way to love
that she knows.

INTO THE SKIES

They left no stones unturned,
to tell a story of their woven lies.
Yet, she stood tall in the dark,
knowing one day she'll touch the skies.

They mistook she'll silently suffer,
only resiliency ignited as paths got rougher.
Shattering the delusions, she felt proud,
once she realized the dreams she vowed.

As sun shines up, her spirit refined,
a reminder of the strength within she confined.
Granted her grace within, kindness remained,
ascending into the skies, the worth she reclaimed.

a poem of renewal

REASONS

You'll naturally find
the courage,
once you become aware
of the reasons
you need it in first place.

HER REALITY

She found her bare truth,
deep in the dark.
The peace and happiness she pursued,
came right on the clock.
It wasn't a mere coincidence to happen,
With strong persistence, it was her true existence
that she constantly fought for.

INTO THE WOODS

Into the woods,
as she wanders,
listening into the silence
of the passing breeze,
her soul starts to swirl
while the mind freeze.
Just being there it felt,
as if the world had
set her free.

a poem of renewal

UNION

Remember, the foremost union
you need is with yourself,
so listen up to you.

UBIQUITOUS LOVE

the light within

Wherever she goes,
she'll always find love,
either within her own sacred space
or some other form,
but it will constantly be around.
With her abiding presence so kind,
it merely desires her acceptance
to welcome it with an open heart
and let that ray of affection shine.

a reflection to remember

SUNSET EMBRACE

The urge to seek validation for one's emotions is often a root cause of the inefficiencies we observe within ourselves. This tendency frequently leads to the belief that we are inadequate, when, in reality, no one, regardless of their closeness or similarity to us, can ever fully comprehend our unique experiences. So, if you continue to wait for an external validation to fully accept what lies within you, it may never happen. The validation you seek from others should emerge from within yourself.

Not every day will feel the same; some days you will be tired at your lowest, while others at your peak, filled with passion and energy. Remember, this journey is like a day from sunrise to sunset, and it needs not be perfect. Just as each day presents a different sunrise, some beautifully painted in hues of pink and yellow, while others obscured by dark clouds and rain, it doesn't remain static; the sunrise will eventually break through. As sun is persistent in gracing the horizon with new rays of sunshine each day, so can you embrace your uniqueness. Similarly, the sunset no matter how dark is purposed to bring utmost rest after the daily turmoils, it is essential that you take that time for yourself, to understand your needs, practice self-love and draw strength from it.

Remember to celebrate both your strengths and flaws and keep taking steps on your journey. Each step you take brings you closer to yourself and may lead to unexpected places. This is the most profound way to nurture self-love and inner peace. Each sunrise and sunset is a part of your beautiful story, so embrace it.

Made in United States
Troutdale, OR
01/26/2024